SEO Marketing Synthesis

Or how to move effectively in the digital world today to propose your products and services

CONDENSED PRACTICAL GUIDE

Rodolfo Turco

First edition

11/11/2020

Copyright© **Rodolfo Turco**

All rights reserved

Google, Microsoft, Bing, **Yahoo**, **Baidu, Apple** are trademarks of their respective owners.

Index

Introduction..5
What is SEO?...7
    Local SEO..9
    Search Engines...10
    Insights...12
Online Marketing..14
    Insights...19
Branding..20
Your Site..22
    Insights...29
Blogs...30
Social Networks...34
Communication channels..36
Information Contents..39
    BackLinks..43
    Insights...44
Images, Video, Audio...45
Linking..49
    Structured Data Markup.......................................53
    Insights...58
Affiliations..59
eCommerce...62
    Insights...66
Competitors...67
Code optimization..70
Useful Resources...75
Glossary..78
The author Rodolfo Turco..80
The Turcotronics company...81

Introduction

This text is a compendium on SEO and Marketing concepts applicable to all products and services provided via the internet, or offline, in the classic market, but advertised and / or sold via the web.

Today, thinking of promoting anything without taking into account how the digital market moves is a commercial suicide, everything revolves around the web, the internet has become the local and global reference point for all activities concerning man and beyond.

In this vademecum I describe the gist of the speech for those who do not have the time and / or the desire to read tomes on the subject, for those who want to take action immediately and for those who want to get a detailed idea in a short time and at an insignificant cost to then perhaps deepen later on the aspects most pertinent to your specific needs, for this purpose in this book you will find a selection of links to resources of Italian and foreign authors, free and not.

Many application details and tricks useful for practical purposes will also be covered to maximize profit in the shortest possible time without neglecting the long-term effects, a vitamin concentrate.

Keep in mind that SEO and Marketing are not exact sciences and depend on many factors, here you will find a solid foundation on which to build and improve your specific business, the market response time is variable from sector to sector, from a few weeks to a few months, so be patient and do not be discouraged, as you must not deceive yourself and stop if you see an immediate fruit, for a lasting harvest it is necessary to improve and stabilize the variables involved, whoever stops is lost.

This guide, being concentrated, is full of concepts that must be internalized, it must be read slowly and with thought, reflecting on each sentence to expand it in the mind and thinking about its applicability in your specific context; it is not a novel, rather a collection of notes, concise and incisive sentences; it is a technical book.

To improve myself in the field of SEO and marketing I had to study a large amount of texts and courses, this took me a lot of time, effort and resources, not having found a complete and at the same time practical excerpt, hence the idea of writing a condensed book starting from the many ideas and notes taken and learned; I hope this synthesis work can help you.

Enjoy the reading,

Rodolfo Turco

What is SEO?

SEO = Search Engine Optimization, or how to maximize your online presence, positioning yourself as high as possible in internet searches.

If the user does not see you in the very first positions of search engines, they will not take you into consideration, you do not exist.

This does not mean being present for everyone but it is essential to be there mainly for that type of users who are your **target**, the too crippled, otherwise it is like having a shop where 1000 people enter a day but almost nobody buys, better to have only 100 but almost all paying customers; the relationship between buyers and visitors is called the **conversion rate**, one of our goals is to maximize it.

How to attract the right people?

We will discuss this throughout the text, we must take care of every aspect, do not neglect the details, for the moment I just mention that we can divide the human race into three categories, relating to your products and services:

1. **Who is not interested**

   It is better to exclude it, it generates traffic not only useless but harmful.

2. **Who might be interested but don't want to buy right away**

   He has to be involved and a job of education has to be done to convince him of the goodness of what you offer, and bring him, sooner or later, into the third category.

3. **Who is looking to buy**

   They are our primary target, we need to maximize their presence and bring them to purchase.

To achieve this, our **goal** must be clear, to understand who the real potential customers are, think how they think and what they will look for, these are our keywords, the key phrases that we must highlight especially in the titles and at the top of our pages.

In the SEO field, the intuitive concept "better reach as many people as possible" is a huge mistake, those who want too much do not squeeze anything, need to focus on the useful goal.

The quality and arrangement of the contents, texts and multimedia parts, images first of all, must be shown, immediately and concisely, the solution to the potential customer's problem, and then give the details, the user must move quickly and easily in the your exposure, always remember that he has no **time** to waste, he wants the solution immediately, if he finds it he will be willing to investigate it, otherwise you have lost it.

Fundamental is the **Brand**, your identifier, the user trusts who he knows, when he needs he could look for you directly by name, and if he sees you in searches he will prefer you; I will detail the topic.

Local SEO

Local SEO is the application of Search Engine Optimization techniques to local businesses such as shops, offices, studios, and any other business that has a well-defined geographical location or in any case a localized area of intervention.

On the net there are several free and paid resources in order to maximize the economic return of your products and services, in this text you will learn the ways.

If you cannot effectively implement all the mechanisms necessary to achieve a concrete result yourself, you can turn to professionals in the sector with a small investment that will have a quick economic return.

In order not to repeat myself, for a description of Local SEO, I refer you to my free eBook **"Local SEO Synthesis"** (Link: https://turcotronics.it/Local SEO Synthesis - Turcotronics.php) here I will detail some implementation aspects that will allow you to optimize your work.

Search Engines

These Big Four represent 95% of the market.

Google is the world leader, we need to focus on him (or is it her?), Without neglecting any other channels relevant to your specific sector.

Microsoft Bing is the second largest channel in the US.

Yahoo, once very relevant, wanted to expand its offer by losing its initial influence, but it is still important.

Baidu is the primary reference point in the Chinese system.

The algorithms of interpretation of user searches are strictly secret, more and more similar to human reasoning but still software, it must be taken into account.

An important concept is indexing, how the engines "remember" the user keywords, we will try to use it to our advantage.

Remember that users are moving mostly towards **smartphones**, it is essential to take this into account for SEO purposes, the display is small and the key information MUST be presented on the front page, no unnecessary burdens, the aesthetics is completely secondary even if in some sectors appearing "professional" can bring advantages, always remember that the user does not have time, if he does not immediately see the solution he goes further, this is also negative because it reduces the **time** spent on your site and the search engine interpret this hit and run as a clear signal that you are not suitable for that specific research and statistically penalizes you, takes you away from the top positions, you become invisible for that key phrase.

An attracted user stays on the site for a long time to learn more, maybe he won't buy, but he will still leave a small footprint in favor of improving your positioning in the search, the higher you are, the more potential customers you will attract and the more you will sell.

An indispensable tool is the **Google Search Console** (Link: https://search.google.com/search-console), improves the performance of your site in Google search and allows you to analyze various parameters useful for SEO.

Another useful tool is **Google Analytics** (Link: https://analytics.google.com), it gives you a lot of information on the progress of your site but requires you to put a small script on the pages to be monitored.

Insights

Free eBook "Local SEO Synthesis" from Turcotronics

Link: https://turcotronics.it/Local_SEO_Synthesis_-_Turcotronics.php

Getting started with search engine optimization (SEO)

Link: https://support.google.com/webmasters/answer/7451184

Google Search Console

Link: https://search.google.com/search-console/about

Google Analytics

Link: https://analytics.google.com

Online Marketing

Whether you already have a business or you want to create a new one, remember that the secret to optimizing results is to **specialize** and **differentiate** yourself, to find your own market **niche** where you can be among the first.

Always focusing on the primary goal, you can then think of increasing profits by offering ancillary or higher-end products and services (upsell).

The temptation to have as large an audience as possible leads to being an indistinguishable drop in the ocean, however, consider that there are billions of people on the internet, so a very selective niche will still be composed of a very large number of potential customers, with the advantage that they will be selected people and already "ready" for your products and services, for them you will be a point of reference.

The selection of people must have similar characteristics and needs, you must solve their specific problems; moreover, the more you specialize, the higher the price of your products and services can be, because you are one of the best in that specific field (for example, few people like Apple as a percentage of the total, but well paying).

Prefer expensive products even if they do not sell much, in this case the quality and presentation must be at the top because very demanding users; or inexpensive but widespread products if you are able to manage large volumes or sell ethereal material (software, eBook, information, music, film), it being understood that a **perceived** high quality product creates a viral effect and sells better; in both cases you need to know the tastes of your niche.

The saying "The customer comes first" always applies, in the sense that people really need to be helped to find the solution they are looking for; often it can be useful to provide them with free valuable material that can be a test of what they can buy, in this way they will be channeled towards the full product or service, this is especially useful for doubters or new customers who do not know you yet .

Gifts of value are very welcome, as a child my parents bought Parmesan cheese by post, the package always contained lots of sweets (high **perceived value** for the target children), we gladly ate cheese; it would have worked with the unpleasant vegetables too.

It is by giving that one receives.

If what you provide is unique or rare you can afford to set high **prices**, you will sell less but better, the actual value depends on various factors and in general it is better to start from a slightly lower number and then go up if there is appropriate demand; on the contrary, if the product / service is common, one must necessarily align with the market, a little less sells better, a little more gives the perception of a better product but then a better service must be provided or it becomes a boomerang.

Being **invasive** has become counterproductive, think about the annoyance of continuous sales phone calls or the mailbox bombarded by SPAM, much better to bring the potential customer to look for you, for this reason it is important to select a narrow target a priori, it is already prepared to follow you, they must see in your offer the answer to their questions.

Advertising is the soul of commerce! Only partially true; maybe in the past; in reality it is unpleasant, often invasive and expensive (films continuously interrupted, internet pages full of stuff that you don't care about and distracts you), those who can afford it must have an adequate return on investment; much better to be able to appear in search engines, this is the soul of SEO, it is free, it is appreciated, it is the user who requested it.

The principle of surveys always applies, we must understand the **real needs** of our whole, our personal tastes are not theirs, today it can be implemented simply by doing intelligent searches on the web, putting yourself in the shoes of those who are looking for us; In this case it is useful to see for each search which terms the engine offers you to complete the sentence you are typing, they are values already written by other users and therefore significant as potential keywords, perhaps secondary ones.

The customer / supplier relationship must be **symbiotic**, you must solve his real problem, he recognizes an economic value to your solution, he was looking for a result and you provided it; the offer must perfectly fit the chosen niche if you are creating a new product / service, or the niche must be selected specifically for what you already own or want to create soon.

A detail to remember is that man often uses **feelings** more than rationality, teasing an emotion is in general more effective than providing coldly technical arguments, this is a little less true for strictly technological objects in which characteristics matter, sometimes even irrationally; however, a good impression, a positive perception of the customer can lead to the purchase more easily.

If you want to create a new work, you need to understand where the market is going, this is why is useful the tool **Google Trends** (Link: https://trends.google.it/trends), which helps you to understand what types of research are done in the world and to be able to understand what the market trend is in a particular sector, if the future projections you will make are right you will be able to anticipate the competition and therefore have a larger slice of the cake; to improve **forecasts** it is advisable to analyze a market that is more responsive to news, for example the USA, Japan, Korea and China for technologies, or other states particularly active in your specific branch; as with viruses, there is always a lapse of time between what appears in one state and propagation in others, so you can play **ahead**.

In summary: attention to the contents and to the perceived quality, which does not mean the measurable one, see youth fashion of tattered trousers; offer and target must be perfectly matched to maximize conversions, sales; be selective and targeted so that the user recognizes you as the best solution; offer an sample that invites them to buy.

To reach potential customers there are various techniques, some as old as the world but still valid, others modern or modernized; **funnels** are in fashion today, new term and implementation for an old concept, we'll see them later; when the number of recipients becomes important, it may be appropriate to automate the mechanism without resulting in spamming, remember that the customer must have the impression that he has searched for you, so he does not feel annoyed and is more inclined to purchase, I will describe the techniques and services ad hoc.

Insights

Google Trends

Link: https://trends.google.it/trends

Google My Business

Link: https://business.google.com

Google Manufacturer Center

https://www.google.com/retail/solutions/manufacturer-center/

Google Merchant Center

https://www.google.com/retail/solutions/merchant-center/

Google Marketing Platform

https://marketingplatform.google.com/

Branding

The brand plays a primary role, it gives you a name, a face, it should also be accompanied by a **motto**, people memorize it more easily than a name, especially if it is original and nice, it must naturally be related to your offer.

It may be appropriate to combine the company's brand with a Personal Brand, a brand associated with yourself, especially for small businesses, you are putting your face on it, you are not an impersonal entity, remember that man is a social animal, recognize the next, and in this case he recognizes you as an **expert** in the sector of his interest; this technique is also useful for larger companies, especially if associated with a specific product or type.

The brand must be made known, this means spreading it but in an intelligent way, resources should not be wasted for a non-specific sowing, whenever possible be targeted, **tune** the channels to your sector, not very effective and expensive to advertise a sewing kit in a automobile magazine.

On the internet there are many different **channels**, each with its own characteristics: news, social media of various types, advertising, experts in moving the masses (influencers), forums, blogs, feeds, linking, local services, we will deepen them all; it is advisable to move on each of them, giving greater emphasis to those that best suit your needs.

Your Site

Your site is the showcase on the world of your business, but like all showcases, not only the aesthetic part must be taken care of but also the functional one, moreover it must be taken into account that to make it effectively "visible" on the internet it must be made "welcome" to the search engines, it is who allow you to find yourself on the net, to do this you need to perfect the composition and contents.

The most appropriate structure to use is the tree one, starting from the main page and branches off to the secondary contents; it is not advisable to have too many ramifications, both the user and the search engine bots will find it more difficult to reach the information they need, three is an optimal value, the user will have to click on at most three links to get to destination, the less the better.

These are the necessary pages:
- **Home page**, the entry point to your site, light, simple, fast but with the necessary for the user to understand what it is about and find the things he expects. In Italy it is mandatory to show the VAT number if you are a company.

- The **Privacy and Cookie policy (GDPR** in Europe), mandatory by law in most states.
- **Contacts,** to be found.
- **Translation** into other languages if you operate in an international context.
- **Who you are**, so that the user knows who he is dealing with.
- **Products, services and content**, your business.

An aspect not to be underestimated is security, for this it is necessary that your site is accessible with the https protocol and has its SSL certificate.

There are various hosting service providers, that is, who host your site, in the free ones the domain displayed in your link will be primarily that of the service provider, for example www.myname.serviceprovider.com, an economical but not very "professional" solution, if you can use your own domain, the annual cost for managing the domain and hosting starts from a few tens of euros, it is worth the expense; in this case you can show your domain, for example www.myname.com

On the internet there are various extensions, the final part of the address after the last point, if possible choose .com because it is perceived better by users, or that of your state, especially if your context is local (.it for Italy).

The files that make up our site can be organized into folders to be sorted, but the rule is always not to exaggerate, better not to nest more than two directory levels.

The file names must be explanatory of the content but not too long, strange characters must be avoided, better to stick to letters, numbers and the minus sign (-), the use of lowercase only is recommended but not essential.

Remember how precious time is, the user does not have to lose, so you must provide him with basic information immediately and then detail later, in this way he will be encouraged to read and consume your content and therefore to stay on your site for a long time, this in addition to increasing the probability of purchase increases the time spent on the site, and this is an important factor for search engines, if the user stays on your site it is a sign that he has found what he was looking for, and the engine will consider your page more for that specific search.

This consideration also applies to the page loading speed, a slow hosting service or heavy pages mean that some users will leave your site before they even read its contents; Search engine bots are also affected because they only give you a small amount of time, and your page loses rank.

To define the writing **styles** we use a particular language called CSS, for convenience you can put the description of the styles in a separate file but this slows down, one more file to load and interpret, if you have few styles you can think of insert them on the same page using the <style> ... </style> construct inside the head <head> ... </head>.

In the chapter on information content we will go into detail on what and how to write on the pages of your site.

Remember that banner ads don't pay off unless you have a flow of visitors of thousands per day, they are just intrusive and annoying.

Several languages are spoken in the world, if you want to show yourself to the world you need a multi-language site, at least in English; there is an automatic page translation tool in many languages provided by Google, it is useful to insert it if you do not have the possibility of manual localization of pages and data in the languages you are interested in; to do this, a small script must be inserted in each page together with a translation button; however, like all scripts, this also slows down, the good thing is that, although it is a very important function it is not used often, you can then adopt a trick to get "goat and cabbage":

normally you should add scripts to your page:

```
<script type="text/javascript">
function googleTranslateElementInit() {
new google.translate.TranslateElement({pageLanguage: 'it'},
 'google_translate_element');
}
</script>

<script type="text/javascript"
  src="//translate.google.com/translate_a/element.jscb=googleTranslateElementInit">
</script>
```

and put the following code where you want the button to appear:

```
<div id="google_translate_element"></div>
```

If you use the following PHP trick you can have the functionality of the Google translate button without increasing the loading time, "normally"; add it where you want the button to appear:

```php
<?php
if ($_GET['Transl'] == "1")
{
echo '<div style="text-align: center;" id="google_translate_element"></div>';
echo '<script type="text/javascript" src="//translate.google.com/translate_a/element.js?cb=googleTranslateElementInit"></script>';
echo '<script type="text/javascript">';
echo 'function googleTranslateElementInit() {';
echo ' new google.translate.TranslateElement({pageLanguage: \'it\'}, \'google_translate_element\');}';
echo '</script>';
} else
{
echo '<a rel="noopener noreferrer nofollow" href="your_page.php?Transl=1" title="Google translate">';
echo '<img src="your_image.png" alt="Google translate" title="Google translate"></a>';
}
?>
```

Where your_page.php is your page to translate and your_image.png is the initial image, which acts as a placeholder, for example an image similar to the button itself, which you can eventually replace with simple text, for example **Translate**, by removing the image from the link.

How does it work:

- when you open your page, the image or text placed as a simple link appears, so the script is not interpreted and loading is fast.

- in the rare case in which the user wants the translation, he presses the link and the same page is called up with the parameter **?Transl=1**

- the page is reopened, but this time the control if($ _GET ['Transl'] == "1") opens it with the translation button itself, in this rare case the user is willing to wait for that second more because it required a specific function indispensable to him.

- At this point the user chooses the language in which to translate and Google translate does the rest.

Measure the speed with the tool

https://developers.google.com/speed/pagespeed/insights/

and you will see a "Time to Interactive", and not only that, much lower than the ordinary use of the script.

The same trick can be used for all those scripts that are used only on request, useless and expensive to interpret them all the time.

Insights

Find out how to make extraordinary sites

Link: https://www.google.it/intl/it/webmasters/learn/

Measure the loading speed of a page

Link:
https://developers.google.com/speed/pagespeed/insights/

Blogs

One of the most effective ways to bring selected customers, and therefore willing to buy, to your shop is to create a blog, that is an article site, relating to topics about your services and products.

The user interested in articles and services that you provide will search the web for information, advice, reviews and anything else that could be useful; if you create good articles on the subject he will be able to find them and therefore be directed towards what you offer.

When you create content, you have to put yourself in the shoes of potential customers and ask yourself the questions to be answered.

There are many ways to create blogs and sites in general, there are pre-built software packages called **CMS**, Content Management System, which make creation easy, fast and very flexible, they are highly customizable, and your site can take on the appearance that most you like and have the features you need, for example an eCommerce.

There are many CMS, both paid and free, but the best known and widespread is **Wordpress** (https://wordpress.org), if you want to create a good blog

I highly recommend using it, this software is free in itself, but to make it work properly it needs a **theme** that creates the appearance of the site, there are free and paid ones, if you want to implement a business solution should focus on professional ones because they are better supported, optimized and updated, prices start from a few tens of euros, therefore affordable, pay close attention to what are the performance in terms of loading the theme, beautiful but slow does not sell, fast and simple yes.

Wordpress also provides expandable basic free hosting with paid features (https://wordpress.com), of course it does not have the performance of a professional service but it is still very good, considering that speed is a fundamental component.

In creating a blog it is advisable to focus and specialize on a single topic, in this way you will attract that particular slice of users who are interested in a special way and therefore more likely to buy; if you want to deal with more topics you can consider having more separate blogs.

Articles particularly welcome are the **tutorials** to explain how to do something, the **review** that describes and evaluates a product or service, a **collection** of objects or resources of a specific type, the **comparison** of several similar things, a detailed **advice** on both what to do and what should be avoided in a certain context; in general, for your specific sector, you have to think about what the user would look for, what he needs, and thus provide a piece written ad hoc to solve his specific problem.

From your blog you can collect the contacts of visitors, typically asking for their name and email and specifying the use that this data will be used for, as example sending new articles, updates on the sector or proposing products and services.

Directly in the article you can suggest your goods, naturally contextualized to the text.

One thing to do when writing new articles is to see if you can link them to articles already written by inserting a link to the old ones, in this way the interested user can read those too.

On Wordpress as on other CMS, you can add features through components called **plugins**, there are all types, including those useful for SEO, both free and paid, but be careful because they could slow down.

As for sites, even on blogs you have to put privacy and cookie policies, as well as the **VAT** number in Italy if you are a company and you trade through them.

On the Wordpress settings you can choose how to store and how to call each new article, it is good that the name is explicit and clear, with a number of folders as little nested as possible to keep the URL at acceptable lengths and above all human readable.

As for sites, **security** is also required for blogs, https must be used by installing an SSL certificate, there are free services that provide it such as Let's Encrypt https://letsencrypt.org/.

The articles must have a length of not less than 2000 words, you have to go into detail and be complete, remember that the first lines make the difference, when possible to outline and help yourself with images.

If the article touches more points, insert an index (**TOC**, Table of Content).

Using engaging language that stimulates curiosity, leads to reflect and ask questions.

Social Networks

Human beings love to socialize, social networks are good collectors of users, also you can create your own discussion groups on a specific topic, speaking as an expert you can give advice and help solve problems, you will have a return of image.

In new groups that are not yours, enter on tiptoe, without spamming, make yourself known first, always stick to your target, to attract people interested in the topics you deal with, those related to your business.

Link the various social networks together, but be careful of those that tend to penalize links like Facebook, better in this case to put links of a discursive type, using keywords, the name of your brand, the primary topic of interest, a motto, image or video.

Users use social media especially to relax, using funny language is of great help; don't obsess them by bombarding them with advertisements.

Youtube: rewards having long videos, at least 10 minutes, keeping attention with frequent scene changes, correlating more videos with each other to increase the visit time; the Youtube platform gives a lot of importance to the time spent on it.

Instagram: its diffusion is growing, users are attracted to photos, especially if they are curious or funny, always put relevant descriptions (hashtags); photos must be original.

Facebook: if possible, add posts in times of less traffic to avoid getting lost in the sea of messages; be concise in the descriptions, a few tens of words, if you need to deepen refer to a blog; stimulating user interaction to be at the top of the messages, is the algorithm behind Facebook, the more a message arouses interest and the higher it is in the ranking.

Forums: a little in decline, but still good when strong interaction is needed, such as asking or answering specific questions; useful to subscribe to those related to your sector, helping when needed. Our own Forum is necessary as a means of supporting our products, often there are people willing to help others

Twitter: when the type of your services offered allows it, for example the information sector, having a channel in which to chirp is useful.

There are several other social networks, some emerging, others widespread only in certain states or very sectorial, choose the ones most similar to your target; as a general rule, it is worth writing to everyone, if only to protect your brand.

Communication channels

To provide your products and services you need to establish a two-way communication with your potential customers, a **symbiosis**.

On the internet it is possible to implement different forms of communication, social media, website, blog, forum, email, telephone, through these channels you can dialogue with words, images and videos.

To be productive, communication must be **discreet**, non-invasive, the user needs to solve a problem, we must help him by proposing our solution.

The buyer must be looking for you, in this way he will already be prepared to buy, propose but not impose himself.

The various transmission pipes must lead to the service or product, all the channels must be linked together (cluster) to achieve this goal, accompany the visitor to the point of interest.

One of the most effective forms, if used correctly, is email, must be requested (Lead Generation) if they want to deepen a concept you have expressed, to get to your product or service.

One way to entice the user to provide you with his data (only Name and eMail) is to provide in exchange articles, free courses, free books (**Lead Magnet**); the content must be of quality, so the potential client can appreciate your work and decide to contact you for his needs.

The data collection pages are called **Squeeze** page or **Optin**, they can be placed with discretion at the top and bottom of each page, or when the user leaves the site; the request form must be very simple: name, email, privacy, enter button.

Remember NOT to spam by sending lotsof emails, always be discreet, send the email only to those who have requested the specific service: news, blogs, product information; annoying the customer is counterproductive, and in the long term it pays off.

The content of the emails must be written carefully, be concise, propose a solution to their specific problem, after all you need to put your data and the possibility to unsubscribe.

Emails can be cognitive like newsletters to keep you informed on news, blog articles to help on specific topics, sales funnels to deliver your products.

Funnels, are a **small** series of emails to lead the customer, especially if undecided, to take an interest in the product; it is not necessary to propose your own solution immediately but to convince him, perhaps with gifts and partial solutions, that you have the solution to their needs, there are specific services to automate this process.

Social media can be used both to propose, to dialogue and help, remember that it is by giving that you receive, similar speech applies to your sites and blogs, useful information is provided for the solution of real problems, forums are suitable for responding to questions and allowing other users to help you find a solution, this is a good way to support your products.

Information Contents

When providing an information product, both free of charge and for a fee, a series of precautions must be followed to obtain a good result, first of all for the user and then for themselves.

The **quality** of the content must be high, do your best to give your best; do not be discouraged if you are not a good writer, I am not, my books will never win a literary prize but I try to give many useful technical details to those who read me; writing must be based on emotions to be persuasive, there are keywords that stimulate the mind of those looking for the **solution** to their problem, use these terms to open the intellect, I list them asking you to stop and reflect on each term: the secret for, effective trick, the mystery of, being positive, obtaining, arriving, discovering, numerical description (schematic listing), technical innovation, exclusive system, advanced course, single method for; when it comes to products: "price", "offer", "discount", "features", "reviews", "buy", "cheap"; use specific terms where applicable, for example "fast", think about the important attributes of your product / service, what sets it apart; more generally you can use: best, opinions, alternative, features, specifications, reviews.

Remember that the more specialized you are, the less competition you have.

The **length** of the content is important, the longer it is the more the user and the search engines will perceive it as complete and decisive, it must of course also have the substance.

For each service offered, a separate page / article must be made, do not try to tell everything about everything in one place.

Find a **slogan** for your company and for your product or service, the mottos are relatively easy to memorize, and if right they lead the user to remember you and to look for you when needed.

When you face the problems, your own and others, you have to take **action** immediately, not be frozen by the fear of making mistakes, a useful tactic for yourself and others is to write eBooks and articles on the things you are knowledgeable about, so you can help those on the subject is less prepared than you, there will always be something you know or know how to do better than others, you can always improve yourself by studying and deepening the topics and thus become an expert on them and be able to share your knowledge and know-how, for free or for reward.

The **title**, the name of what is presented is fundamental, for the angels it is even their purpose, their mission, so think of something representative without going into the obvious, the banal, the usual, always stand out but synthesize the content, the title is a primary search key, the keyword par excellence.

The introduction is the most important part of the text, video or any other form of communication, users must immediately give the impression that they have found what they were looking for, so they will be encouraged to deepen.

To achieve the goal you need to use your knowledge and experience, describe the best way to get to a result, the mistakes made and how they were remedied, use concrete evidence, state what are the pros and cons, use application examples, compare solutions, put a glossary of technical terms to help newbies, stimulate them to move towards a solution, give more choice to meet slightly different needs, refer to articles that prove your solution; post or link testimonials to corroborate your point of view; the problem solved for one person could be of help to others who have similar problems, so describe your competence to be considered an expert in the field.

At the end of everything you need to take **action** (call to action), which can be a further study, a free or paid offer, have the customer leave the data (name and email).

In the text the **keywords** must be put, which are nothing more than the typical phrases that a person would search for on the internet, these hooking points will be used by search engines to get to your content and therefore indirectly to your services and products; the main keyword must be repeated every hundred words, synonyms and related phrases must also be used; better to use short **phrases** than single words (long tail keywords) because the more specific you are, the more likely you are to end up on the first page of the search, for common words and phrases instead you have no chance.

Useful is Google's keyword planning tool (Link: https://ads.google.com/home/tools/keyword-planner/), which allows you to search and verify the most appropriate sentences for your context.

Search the keywords, and phrases related to your topic on Google and other search engines to see what searches suggest in the dropdown that opens, you can use those phrases in the text because they are keywords already searched by users; occasionally use bold and other mediums to highlight and stand out, but don't overdo it.

The links to your **contacts** must be clearly visible, so that if the user is willing to look for you, he can easily find you.

I repeat it several times so that it becomes fixed in your mind, it is of great importance to be single topic, selective, specialized, to have a specific target, talking about everything at all does not make you an expert in anything, if you have more skills and want to make them available consider the hypothesis of having more specialized sites; you will attract a very specific and interested audience, so you can help her better and she will help you; this also applies to the topics covered, do not put too much meat on the fire, just describe the solutions to a specific problem, then if you have other related but independent arguments then write separately on the latter and link to the antecedent ones, for example you talk about a coffee machine, deepen that, do not discuss in detail the pods, make an in-depth article on pods and link the two texts; in the article on coffee machines do not also mention blenders and citrus juicers, much less flower pots.

I suggest Neilpatel Ubersuggest to do an analysis of the content posted online (free and paid, Link: https://app.neilpatel.com/).

BackLinks

An important aspect for Local SEO as well as for the global one is the addressing by other sites to ours, the backlinks, these allow us to give notoriety to our site and will be considered by search engines as a relevant element for the purposes of ranking, positioning in the results provided.

We will discuss the topic in a dedicated chapter.

Insights

Neilpatel Ubersuggest online content analysis

Link: https://app.neilpatel.com/

Google's keyword planner

Link: https://ads.google.com/home/tools/keyword-planner/

Images, Video, Audio

The image is a powerful means of communication, both in static and video form, in some contexts even the audio is fundamental, but it should not be used as background music on the sites, I recommend, you would antagonize people.

There are **free** image providers on the internet, make sure they are truly distributable, preferably in the Public Domain (CC0 license or similar), others can also be bought and distributed under certain conditions, below is a non-exhaustive list of sites:

https://unsplash.com/

http://pickupimage.com/

https://picjumbo.com/

https://digitalcollections.nypl.org/

http://publicdomainvectors.org/

https://stocksnap.io/

https://pixabay.com/it/

http://skuawk.com/

http://www.splitshire.com/

http://www.lifeofpix.com/

https://www.pexels.com/

http://gratisography.com/

Those who can and know how to do it, better photograph them by themselves, and are sure of the originality as well as the representativeness of what you want to describe, this is essential for the items that are sold, no eye examination miniatures, clear images and contextualized to the use of the product.

Even for videos and sounds, you have to be careful with copyright in order to avoid unnecessary hassle and respect the rights of others.

The videos on the pages of the sites must be used in moderation because they are heavy, avoid autoplay, unpleasant to most, leave the user the freedom to decide, the impositions are always deleterious.

Of course, **multimedia** content must be adherent and consistent with the topic.

Another very welcome visual representation are diagrams, graphs, tables, everything that can be of support to our arguments.

For all object formats it is necessary to use representative names, no to video123, image27, but a concise description of the content, using the keywords; also insert an appropriate caption.

If you create the contents yourself the speeches made for the texts are worth, only the information communication channel changes, but the techniques are the same; the first part is important, there are those who use the APP scheme (Agree, Promise, Preview), agree to the problem, promise and anticipate the solution, but it depends on the descriptive context; don't be boring, moving the scene increases attention and memorization, a duration of 10 minutes is ideal if the video is the primary medium, but it can be much shorter depending on what you are communicating, for example the descriptions videos of specific passages in a text should be concise, they are only supportive.

Videos as a primary means of communication must be accompanied by slides, handouts, texts, to provide details at hand; the video communicates better but the writing is more practical to search and use the single data.

In general, communication can be mixed, text, image, audio, video as long as it is harmonious, the goal is always to communicate a message in the most effective way possible; sympathy always works, funny and spectacular videos are the most popular on Youtube.

The resolution of the images and videos must be designed for the transmission medium, usually the mobile phone, therefore neither too high, it would not be useful and would be heavier, nor of low quality to be unpleasant or illegible.

As for texts, multimedia contents must also be connected, linked to related topics, whatever the means of communication used to describe them, this will allow the user to deepen, if he wishes, and will also increase the time spent in our channels, this it applies both between the various internal documents and for external links, for example social networks or other sites.

Linking

Links are the main mechanism by which information is accessed on the internet; the various sites, and the pages in them, are linked through links, for this reason their care and management is of particular importance, both for those inside and outside their sites.

The principle is that the more our data is linked **externally**, the greater the probability of being found by potential customers; our links must be present in search engines and other sites relevant to the arguments we deal with.

The **internal** links to their sites are used to correlate products and articles, as well as the sites laid out if you have more than one, for example if it is vacuum cleaners you can link to your bags, if you are talking about robots connect the download of the related updates software; this allows the user to navigate within our data structure to obtain products, services and notions they need; among these are the Breadcrumbs, the sequence of connections in the tree hierarchy of our pages, for example home-> computers-> laptops.

The external links are used to link other sites with information, services and products relevant to our business, among these there are also affiliations with third-party companies; the aim is always to provide users with a service that in any case produces a return, not necessarily of an economic nature, in which we are interested; for the names of external links avoid the use of keywords of your own interest because otherwise you lead the search engine to link them to sites that are not yours; if you have several sites, you must clearly tie them together.

The external links to our sites (**backlinks**) are those that can lead potential visitors to our content, these links represent a very important source and can be obtained in various ways, social networks, advertising (in moderation), sites that deal with topics similar to ours, sites with similar activity lists, product sales sites where we expose ours, in general any external source that may be related to us in order to bring traffic into target.

How to find them? Just do a search as if you were looking for yourself, exclude those who are your competitors, and consider the rest.

Always put the target="_ blank" attribute in external links so that the browser opens a new page and yours still remains open.

One technique is to provide blogs or sites that deal with topics related to ours with quality **articles** (guest posts) in which our link is present with our brand in the link name, if the blogger finds the content interesting decide to publish it, of course we can return the favor; our products can also be presented but enhancing the response to a need of others.

The greater the authority of the site hosting our links, the greater the probability that a user decides to visit us; if we have an activity it is appropriate to be present in the various specialized sites that list the activities if you have a local business it is useful to have the name of the city in the link.

Search engines are nothing more than services that provide links to information that the user needs, so it is important that the name of the file that appears in the **URL** (the full path to our page) must be explanatory of the content, even the content folders must be significant and as little as possible nested so as to have a modest length and the links are easily readable and interpretable by humans and machines (search engine indexing bots).

The anchor text associated with the link is also important and must be descriptive, this applies to both internal and external links, so for example if you want to provide software for home loans, do not write "download the software from the following link" but "download the software for calculating the mortgage", which then in HTML will take a form of the type

<a href="https://www.mysite.com/download/mortgage-calculation-software.zip"> Mortgage calculation software </a>.

This way the search engine will know what it is and can index it.

Structured Data Markup

The search engines, in addition to using the data explicitly shown in the pages of the websites, use data not visible to the user, but present in the same pages, provided that you put them there, called "Structured Data Markup", these data are declared in the HEAD at the top of the pages, for clarity I insert them just before </head>.

The schema used by this data is that https://schema.org/ and the preferred format is JSON-LD.

These structured texts are used to inform the engine about the contents on the page and must be consistent with them; for example you can describe an organization, a person, a restaurant, a recipe, a book, the types of data that can be described are many, refer to the links included for an exhaustive list; from this Markup the search engine can understand in a rigorous way how the data are structured and can therefore present them in the correct form; here I bring some practical examples:

Page Breadcrumb

```
<head>
... omissis ...
  <script type="application/ld+json">
  {
   "@context": "https://schema.org",
```

```
    "@type": "BreadcrumbList",
    "itemListElement": [{
      "@type": "ListItem",
      "position": 1,
      "name": "Turcotronics",
      "item": "https://turcotronics.it/"
    },{
      "@type": "ListItem",
      "position": 2,
      "name": "Increase the number of your customers",
      "item": "https://turcotronics.it/how to increase customers.php"
    }]
  }
</script>
</head>
```

Organization description

```
<script type="application/ld+json">
  {
    "@context": "https://schema.org",
    "@type": "Organization",
    "address": {
      "@type": "PostalAddress",
      "addressLocality": "Milazzo, Italia",
      "postalCode": "98057"
    },
    "email": "informa@turcotronics.it",
    "alumni": [
```

```
    {
      "@type": "Person",
      "name": "Rodolfo Turco"
    }
   ],
   "name": "Turcotronics",
   "telephone": "+39 3484504760",
   "url": "https://turcotronics.it",
   "logo": "https://turcotronics.it/immagini/TuT.png"
  }
</script>
```

Person description

```
<script type="application/ld+json">
  {
    "@context": "https://schema.org",
    "@type": "Person",
    "email": "mailto: informa@turcotronics.it",
    "image": "immagini/Rodolfo.jpg",
    "jobTitle": "Turcotronics CEO",
    "name": "Rodolfo Turco",
    "telephone": "+39 3484504760",
    "url": "https://www.turcotronics.it/"
  }
</script>
```

Video description

\<script type="application/ld+json"\>
   {
    "@context": "https://schema.org",
    "@type": "VideoObject",
    "thumbnailUrl": "./immagini/Sintesi-SEO-Marketing.jpg",
    "contentUrl": "video-corso-seo-marketing-turcotronics.php"
    "uploadDate": "2020-11-11",
    "name": "SEO Marketing Video Course",
    "description": "Video Course on SEO and Marketing to improve your online business.",
    "author": {
       "@type": "Person",
       "name": "Rodolfo Turco"
    }
   }
\</script\>

Book description

\<script type="application/ld+json"\>
   {
    "@context": "https://schema.org",
    "@type": "Book",
    "bookFormat": "EBook",
    "copyrightHolder": {
     "@type": "Person",
     "name": "Rodolfo Turco"

```
  },
  "copyrightYear": "2020",
  "description": "Local SEO Synthesis",
  "inLanguage": "it",
  "name": "Local SEO Synthesis",
  "publisher": {
    "@type": "Organization",
    "name": "Turcotronics"
  }
}
</script>
```

As you can see, a hierarchical structure and specific tags are used to indicate each element of detail, at the link https://developers.google.com/search/docs/guides/intro-structured-data find a helpful introduction article.

To validate the correctness of the structures you create you can use different online tools, I point out that of Google https://search.google.com/structured-data/testing-tool

With this mechanism it is also possible to insert multimedia data, the search engine, at its discretion, can use them to improve the user experience and thus show results relevant to what it is looking for; to validate this data you can use the tool https://search.google.com/test/rich-results

Insights

Scheme used in the Structured Data Markup

Link: https://schema.org/

Recommended data format in Structured Data Markup

Link: JSON-LD Linked Data format

Introduction to structured data

Link: https://developers.google.com/search/docs/guides/intro-structured-data?hl=it

Structured data testing tool

Link: https://search.google.com/structured-data/testing-tool

Multimedia data test tool

Link: https://search.google.com/test/rich-results

Affiliations

A trading method as old as the world is to sell the products and services of others, this is the classic case of the local shop, but it can also be implemented on the internet in different ways including direct eCommerce, the Dropshipping which I will talk about in chapter on eCommerce, and Affiliations.

Affiliation means the proposal of something physically sold by others, the user buys through your advice without spending anything more but sometimes getting discounts, while you, the affiliate, get a part of the seller's revenues for having procured him the customer; sometimes the term **Referral** is also used.

Many companies offer affiliate programs, many famous as Amazon and Google, others less known; a careful selection must be made, choosing only those companies that offer quality services and products with seriousness, this is because you put your face on it, something is recommended; in my personal experience I have signed up for dozens of affiliate programs but less than a third have passed the exam, and not all with flying colors, for professional ethics, when I propose something I explicitly write that it is affiliation and I put some clarifying notes where I deem it necessary.

Affiliate programs should be chosen in relation to what you offer or what you are an expert on, and only on things that you know well from direct experience.

The commissions obtained from the affiliations vary a lot, from a few percentage points to the entire share, whether it is convenient or not should be evaluated from time to time, not always a higher percentage corresponds to a higher profit, it depends on how much the product can be sold through your channel; those who are experts in tires and suggest vegetables will hardly be convincing, but if they suggest that tire model of that brand because it is fitted in their car then the customer has more faith in the advice.

You can reverse it and create **your own** affiliate program, in which case others will propose your products and services, and in exchange for the customers they will provide you will recognize them a part of your income; if even the big names in electronic commerce use this technique, it is a clear sign that the mechanism works and brings benefits.

Whether side you are on affiliation, there are services on the net that allow you to join or offer the affiliation, this relieves the management part but of course the service has a cost, usually a percentage on the transaction; nothing detracts from the fact that you can do everything yourself.

For example my affiliation to ShareASale
https://www.shareasale.com/

For Wordpress and the main eCommerce software there are plugins that allow you to insert affiliations with a certain configurability.

Whether you have a blog or an ordinary site, you can dedicate a space for each affiliate program where the pros and cons are described for clarity to the user.

Useful documentation can be found on the Amazon affiliate site

https://amazon-affiliate.eu/

eCommerce

The Internet is a huge market, you can buy and sell anything.

It can be a great showcase for your local business, as an opportunity to do old and new jobs exclusively online, the possibilities are many and there is room for almost any job, whatever your propensity as a novice or a veteran business.

There are several possibilities to implement an e-commerce, I describe the main ones:

Direct and indirect trade from your site

You can implement an online store by having a website and inserting free software that allows you to create a store, the most famous are WooCommerce and PrestaShop, but there are others.

In your shop you can sell both your own products and services and the products of others whose goods you have in stock if they are physical, and the products of others in dropshipping, i.e. selling from your site but automatically placing the order in turn on another shop by putting the shipping address of the final customer, in this case you do not have your own warehouse but you still have to manage sales and assistance; for dropshipping it is advisable to rely only on shops that have a local warehouse, for example a European one for Italy, otherwise the shipping times are really long, from China typically exceeding a month, and in times of crisis, such as that generated from the COVID-19 virus, they don't come at all.

Trade from other sites

Your products and services can be sold on other sites such as Amazon, eBay, Google or Apple, depending on the type of goods offered; you can also propose your material to online shops specialized in your sector, there are all kinds of them, just do a targeted search on the internet.

In any case, whatever form you take, it is always necessary to make your presence felt online through the means described in this book, i.e. ordinary website, blog, social network, email, advertising (with moderation and intelligence or you go at a loss) and all other forms of electronic communication; if potential customers do not find you they certainly do not buy, this is why SEO and Marketing techniques must be applied well, the more you optimize the better the chances of success.

For those who are beginners and do not yet have their own product but want to try their hand in the internet world, I recommend starting with a simple ecommerce site, a blog and digital products such as eBooks, videos and courses (**infoproducts**), if you have any **skill** it is time to make them profitable (artistic works, manufacturing of objects, whatever you are better than average at); to start you don't need money or just a few, as you have more financial resources you can access more advanced paid services, therefore more performing and effective, so as to gradually increase income, of course if you start with an initial investment has greater possibilities and faster growth, but if you can't, don't be discouraged, many billionaires have done their job, they started in a humble and simple way, if the idea is good and there is commitment, over time they will also show results; we are all experts in something, you don't need to be geniuses, you just need to be more prepared than the average in a sector, moreover you can always improve by studying, you will be able to offer something concrete to those who, in that specific sector, are less prepared or are looking for the object you have created, it is the classic case of who is a teacher, they are not born there, they study, learn and transmit as best they can what have learned, or the case of the craftsman who creates and he sells the fruit of his labor; giving online lessons is also a method of rounding up; dropshipping is another opportunity to consider; affiliations and referrals allow for additional revenue.

Specializing in a specific sector is very important, you will have less competition, you will be considered experts and therefore you will have more possibilities, remember that even a small niche, being the internet very extensive, can still contain a critical mass of users, sufficient to create a good income; to this primary activity you can add the side services, always relevant to your sector, useful for increasing and stabilizing revenues.

The Internet can and must also be the showcase for your local businesses, whether you have a shop, office, company or whether you are a service provider without a physical location, being present on the net has become essential, your direct competition does and if you do not adapt, you are cut off, you lose ground, you lose customers, you have to adapt to every change or you become extinct, dinosaurs, despite being big and strong, no longer exist; in this regard, read my free book **"Local SEO Synthesis"**

Link: turcotronics.it/Local SEO Synthesis - Turcotronics.php

Insights

Woo Commerce

https://woocommerce.com/

Presta Shop

https://www.prestashop.com/

My free book "Local SEO Synthesis"

turcotronics.it/Local SEO Synthesis - Turcotronics.php

Competitors

Each market has many figures who provide the same products and services, if not the same, certainly similar; there is not a single plumber nor a single computer salesman, if you are reading this book it means that even in your sector you are not the only operator, there is competition.

Just think for a moment that you're the **only** house painter in your city, wouldn't that be nice?

You would always have work and could raise the price of the service.

To achieve this, or at least get close to it, you must specialize, have a field of intervention and therefore a target of restricted, elite users, there you will be the only one or one of the few, with all the advantages that this entails; of course you still need to have a sufficient catchment area, and this is easy on the internet, it is much less if you work in a small town and sell only locally, so the sector to choose should be well thought out if your area is strictly local, in this case it is necessary to differentiate the offer.

Another solution is to be the best in the industry, who wants the best, and is therefore willing to pay more, must call you.

But how to be the best?

The answer is similar to the previous one, differentiating itself, providing what a specific circle is looking for, in that specific sector there are few, if not the only suppliers, so it is much easier to be the best or among the very first.

If you are unable to achieve the above, you can always try to get closer to the ideal situation, an obvious technique is to analyze what the competitors offers, do a search, see what they provide and how they do it the first on the list, try to achieve something better in one or more important aspects, apply the correct SEO and marketing techniques and try to climb the top, if what you create has an interesting aspect that others do not have, here those who appreciate that detail will prefer you.

Of course you have to be realistic and concrete, if you have just opened your online shop and you think you are competing with Amazon you have very little chance, foresight is a good thing but dreams, immediately, do not fill your stomach or pay the bills; you have to start moving where you have real short-term possibilities without neglecting future developments.

An important factor is the price, if there are few or if you are really better than the average you can raise it, otherwise you have to conform to the market.

Analyze every aspect of the competitors that is in front of you, characteristics of the products, price, related services, strengths and weaknesses, customer opinion, marketing methods, communication systems, keywords used; if on the first search page you find results that do not belong to competitors, you can check if they can bring you advantages by offering them a symbiosis, a mutual advantage, what is not against you can be brought in your favor.

Code optimization

Whatever the content and architecture used on your site you need to pay attention to SEO optimization and loading speed.

The site must be pleasant but light, the heavier it is and the more the user experience is negatively affected, people care very little about it being super beautiful, they need the information and they need it immediately, a large percentage of users leave the site earlier even that everything opens because it is slow; others, me first, come out immediately as soon as they see it full of advertisements and popups, annoying sites to read, I close and look elsewhere, and so will your visitors.

Remember that now most of the searches and views are done from smartphones, so small screen and low computing power, the site must necessarily be optimized for mobile phones, Google was very clear about it.

The lack of SEO optimization significantly penalizes the positioning in search engines and the user simply does not find you, you do not exist, maybe you are on the fourth page, but how many go there?

Below I describe simple but necessary optimizations to be made on the files of your site; if you have direct access to the files it will be easy, a little more difficult for CMS-based sites like Wordpress and others, but there are plugins that simplify the task.

First you need the meta **viewport** to adapt the page to the mobile phone screens.

<meta name="viewport" content="width=device-width, initial-scale=1">

The meta **title** must be between 30 and 60 characters and preferably contain your Brand; because that's what the user sees in searches.

The meta **description** must be between 70 and 150 characters, the primary keywords go there.

The meta **keyword** must not have duplicate keys, do not overdo the list, it is not necessary.

The **H1** titles must not be duplicated with the meta title and description, do not do wild copy and paste, preferably it must have a greater detail of the meta title.

H2 titles are also important, albeit secondary, use them and keep them under 70 characters.

The **number** of words on the page must be sufficiently high, about 2000 words, with the primary and secondary keywords well distributed; this is not always possible to do on the front page, because for presentation reasons it is generally more sober than the others.

The **anchor text** of links and images must be descriptive and clear to the user and the bots.

The **URL** of the page must be kept under 55 characters, all inclusive, so a few nestings of folders and file names that are significant but not kilometers.

Style CSS files have a big impact on loading times, if possible, although it is more onerous to keep putting the bare essentials inline to the page via <style> ... </style>.

Another brick are the **scripts**, use those really necessary, where possible load them deferred or on user request, in this text I have explained a technique.

The obtaining email page should be on its own, so that the captcha script does not burden the first page, which is the most important; in general try to **spread** the load across multiple pages rather than putting everything on one.

Limit advertising and videos to the maximum, keep images at a low resolution but not so much that they are grainy, formats with good compression and recent should be used.

Compact (minifier) the code by removing everything that is not necessary. The CMS theme makes the difference, non-optimized themes are slow, the loading time must be one of the primary choice parameters.

For CMS there are various SEO **plugins** that allow you to set the listed parameters, search for them in the list of plugins, there are free and paid, Yoast SEO is the best known.

For content analysis use sites such as Neilpatel Ubersuggest that allow you to find SEO errors, https://app.neilpatel.com/

To test the speed of the site and the CMS themes there are several tools, I propose the following sites:

Google PageSpeed Insights

https://developers.google.com/speed/pagespeed/insights/

Pingdom Website Speed Test

https://tools.pingdom.com/

GTmetrix

https://gtmetrix.com/

These software allow, in addition to measuring the speed, to understand which are the components that slow down the most, eliminate the unnecessary ones and optimize the rest; typically these are CSS scripts and style sheets.

Other notes on speed

The choice of **hosting**, the service that hosts the site, is fundamental, a few tens of euros more on a good one can make the difference, choose it according to the countries in which you want to be present, a local hosting can be more efficient than a faster but foreign one if you want to be present above all in a specific state or continent; for my sites I have chosen an Italian service with a European extension, I propose the link to my affiliation:

VHosting, European hosting based in Italy

If I need to be present in another specific state or continent, I do local searches.

If possible, avoid **redirecting** pages, especially the first one; insert all your links with the www and set the site according to agreement, it is used by the CDN (Content Delivery Network), you avoid having to convert sitename.com into www.sitename.com

Using **caches**.

Set page **compression**.

Using **CDNs**, Cloudflare is the best known, if you want to be fast enough even in states where your hosting has no datacenters.

Useful Resources

From Turcotronics

Free eBook "Local SEO Synthesis"

Link: https://turcotronics.it/Local SEO Synthesis - Turcotronics.php

Products, services, offers and free material

Link: https://www.turcotronics.it

Blog articles to keep informed

Link: https://www.turcotronics.com

From Google

Getting started with search engine optimization (SEO)

Link: https://support.google.com/webmasters/answer/7451184

Find out how to make extraordinary sites

Link: https://www.google.it/intl/it/webmasters/learn/

Find out how to make extraordinary sites

Link: https://search.google.com/search-console/about

Google Analytics, in-depth analysis of the performance of your site

Link: https://analytics.google.com

Keyword Planner

Link: https://ads.google.com/home/tools/keyword-planner/

Google My Business

Link: https://business.google.com

Google Manufacturer Center

https://www.google.com/retail/solutions/manufacturer-center/

Google Merchant Center

https://www.google.com/retail/solutions/merchant-center/

Google Marketing Platform

https://marketingplatform.google.com/

From other sources

Neilpatel Ubersuggest online content analysis

Link: https://app.neilpatel.com/

Let's Encrypt

Link: https://letsencrypt.org/ SSL certificate

Glossary

Affiliation Commercial collaboration for the proposal of products and services

App Software application on mobile

Blog Site of informative articles on a specific topic

Bot Automatic software that performs an action, such as looking for something

Dashboard Control panel

Directory Folder: site that lists activities

Domotic Home automation

eBook Electronic book readable on mobile phones, computers and ad hoc devices

Feedback Retroactive effect of a message or action

Funnel Technique to bring customers to your business

Hosting Service that hosts the data of your website

NAP Name Address Phone

Post Article, review

Referral Commercial collaboration for the proposal of products and services

SEO Search Engine Optimization

SSL Secure Sockets Layer: safety certificate

Structured data Information that describes the structure of something (person, video, organization, ...)

TOC Table of Content: index

Web Network of connections

The author Rodolfo Turco

He has been working for over 30 years in the IT, electronic, automation and plant engineering fields, he is the owner of Turcotronics.

Graduated in automatic electronics, specialization in computer science, since his university days in computer engineering he has been involved in teaching, software, hardware, plant engineering and automation, both for some companies and for himself.

Link to Curriculum Vitae

The Turcotronics company

It provides technological services for the home, shop, office and business.

It is oriented towards smaller realities, from domestic users to small businesses, even if it occasionally collaborates with large companies.

Creation of websites, services, courses and internet consultancy, SEO, Marketing.

Software and firmware development on Windows, Linux, Android, Microcontrollers, PLC.

Computers, Mobile Phones, Networks, TV, Audio / Video, Electronics maintenance and assistance.

Home and industrial automation, Amazon Alexa®, Google Home®.

Electronic, electrical, hydraulic and thermal systems.

General repairs in the home, office, shop.

Repetitions and courses, technical and scientific subjects.

Site: turcotronics.it

Blog: turcotronics.com

www.ingramcontent.com/pod-product-compliance
Lightning Source LLC
Chambersburg PA
CBHW070450220526
45466CB00004B/1792